Inside Summerhill

JOSHUA POPENOE

with candid photographs by the author

Hart Publishing Company, Inc. · New York City

To Neill, with love

The author carrying a little friend

Inside Summerhill

HOW I CAME TO SUMMERHILL

MY FATHER WAS with the Peace Corps, and when he was sent to Malaysia for two years in 1963, we, his family, of course, went along with him. My younger brother and I attended a rather strict English-run school. My oldest sister got the worst deal. She was sent to an all-girls convent school, the only school that would accept her. Janina was absolutely miserable.

One day, she came across a magazine which contained an article about Summerhill. She had previously read the book. She swore—in the manner good little convent girls are supposed to swear—she would go there. So she wrote Neill, though without much hope of being accepted.

Neill's reply was typical:

5 Feby, 1964

"Dear Janina,

So your convent school is very strict. I thought that convents were following Jesus who loved children. Dear me! Summerhill has no religion, yet every child loves it.

We are full up, but there is a chance that a bed for a girl your age may be vacant when we open again in May. But it is a long and expensive way from Malaysia to here, unless of course, you walk and swim it.

Let me know soon because lots want to come here. Already we have twenty-eight Americans and we are trying to learn their language; but I cain't yet call a bawth a beth or a dawnce a dence, but I do know a sparrow is a little boid.

Cheerio,
Neill."

So Janina went to Summerhill. Every letter we received from her was filled with nothing except how much she adored the place. She threatened that if my parents didn't send my brother and me there, she would never forgive them as long as she lived.

In 1965, after my father's term in Malaysia was over, he debated whether to go to England and study for a doctorate, or to return to the United States. One factor influencing his decision was that if he went to England we would be able to go to Summerhill, although, at the time, he wasn't quite sure that he believed in *all* of Neill's ideals.

So we went to live in England. One of the first things we did was visit Summerhill.

MY FIRST VISIT TO THE SCHOOL

ON THE BASIS of that one visit, if I had not been continuously pushed by my sister to enroll in Summerhill, I probably never would have. The physical aspects of the place were not in any way what I had imagined. The name *Summerhill* had led me to think of beautiful meadows and fields with flowers everywhere. I envisioned gorgeous, sunny weather, and a place where no

INSIDE
SUMMERHILL
11

one was ever unhappy. In reality, the grounds and buildings looked slightly shabby, though in a friendly, rather than in a foreboding, way.

Being a fairly unhappy boy of about eleven with a slight inferiority complex about my height, I was very nervous when I visited the school. I was ready to enlarge any small unfavorable incident to an immense degree. And several such incidents did occur.

First, there was the general attitude of the kids and staff towards us—and to any visitors at all, for that matter. The kids either completely ignore visitors, or try to cadge sweets and money off of them, or act obnoxious in an obvious way. This kind of greeting was not the slightest bit encouraging to me, and it made all of us feel as if we were intruding into their privacy—which in fact we were.

Another reason I felt out of place was because I was dressed neatly with a tie, fancy trousers, etc., while the Summerhill kids were all wearing comfortable blue jeans and baggy sweaters. Worse still, during most of my visit, some stupid-looking girl—at the ripe old age of eleven, I thought all girls were stupid-looking—kept following me around asking me all sorts of annoying questions like who was I, and was I going to be at Summerhill next term. To top it all off, when I went looking for my sister to say goodbye, some boy of about sixteen or seventeen came up and asked me what I was "doing around here anyway" and then roughed me up a bit. I ran away crying.

As you can imagine, these experiences did not exactly endear the place to my heart. Yet, because of Janina's rapturous reports, I thought there must be something to Summerhill after all, so I decided to try it for a term of three months.

MY FIRST TERM AT SUMMERHILL

MY FIRST TERM was pretty miserable, as it is with so many of the kids coming to Summerhill for the first time. Even though my parents were good liberals of the day—whatever that means —I had never experienced total freedom before—at least not the Summerhill brand. And so my first year was mostly spent in "breaking out," as they call it—and this doesn't mean with pimples. "Breaking out" means breaking all the codes of conduct that society tries to enforce on us kids.

My breaking out stage was fairly gentle compared to some that Summerhill has seen. When some kids, who come from relatively strict families discover the freedom of Summerhill, they turn around and smash up the place. In many cases, this behavior comes about because the kid thinks there are strings attached to his freedom, which is the way his life was organized prior to his entering Summerhill. "Daddy will take you swimming, IF you clean up your room." Or "You can go out and play football, IF you wash the dishes." Usually, the more tempting the promise, the longer the strings.

So when a kid comes to Summerhill where he can do completely as he likes, he smashes the place, or he becomes antisocial in some other way—*just to find out what the strings really are.* He must discover the limits of acceptable behavior and the payment for over-stepping.

But there ARE no strings.

One new kid started smashing windows just to test reactions, and to find out if the school *really* was free. He was heartily encouraged by Neill to continue. Neill complained to that kid that he hadn't broken enough windows, and that his aim was terrible.

This reaction from the headmaster was the last one the kid expected from an adult. It really shocked him. But that kid learned that he would not be punished. The only punishment he received was self-inflicted, in that he had to sleep in his cold room for a couple of nights until the windows were mended.

Many other kids, of course, were not particularly

overjoyed at having to sleep in a cold room, but the majority of them didn't say anything. Summerhill kids are remarkably tolerant towards this kind of behavior by new students, because Summerhill kids realize that they themselves went through the very same stage when they first came to the school. And they know that it's usually only a matter of time until the new kid settles down.

I can't remember doing anything really drastic in the way of breaking out, but I do remember that I had certain misconceptions about freedom, which I demonstrated by carving my initials deep into the good mahogany staff room table, because I thought I could do anything I wanted. I was severely reprimanded by Ena (Mrs. Neill) who scared the hell out of me.

THE DINING-ROOM ARRANGEMENTS

I WAS SLIGHTLY paranoid when I first came to Summerhill. Many little incidents made me feel miserable and unliked. One such occurrence concerned something as unimportant as meal-seating arrangements.

In Summerhill, the dining room is not big enough to hold all the kids at one time, so lunch and supper are served in shifts. All the younger kids, up to the 12-year-olds, eat first. Then, the others come in and eat, after the younger ones have cleared out.

Now when you're a border-line case, it makes you feel really great to eat with the staff and the older kids. I was going to turn twelve in about a week, and I was excited about going into second lunch and second supper. But a meeting was held, and the majority decided that the second shift was already too full. So they raised the age of entry to thirteen.

I was pretty angry, but I resolved to suffer in silence and wait until I turned thirteen. When I reached thirteen, I triumphantly entered the second meal shift. Then another meeting was called, because now there were too many kids in the first shift. The majority decided that the age should be lowered back to twelve. This really hurt my pride and I took it personally. I don't think I talked to anybody for the rest of the week.

MY HEIGHT GIVES ME TROUBLE

ANOTHER INCIDENT which hurt me quite a bit was when one of the teachers who was going to give classical guitar lessons to some of the kids would not let me join, because, he said, I was too small to handle the instrument well, even though I had already been playing the guitar for a year. There were other kids of my own age in that particular class. This decision was distinctly un-Summerhillian in attitude. The usual action is to let the kid try it, and to let him discover for himself whether he can or can't do it.

Apparently, one of the main reasons that I had a lousy time during the early months of my stay was because I was always trying to assert my superiority over everybody to make up for my height, or at any rate, my lack of it. Of course, if someone had told me that at the time I probably would have bopped him one on the nose.

RAIDING THE KITCHEN

SEVERAL TIMES during my first year, I was quite jealous because I didn't have the nerve to be as anti-social as some of my contemporaries. This defect in my personality came to light mainly when I faced the opportunity to break into the kitchen and steal food. People argue that in a free school one should leave things unlocked and trust the children. A dandy theory,

but in practice—free school or not—most of the food would be taken. It would be an insane thing to leave the kitchen unlocked. Of course, locks don't stop some clever little thieves, and the kitchen gets rifled all the same. Though, usually, only small quantities of food are stolen.

I don't think there is a boy in the history of Summerhill over the age of twelve who did not break into the kitchen at least once, most of the time as much for the adventure as for the food. Most of the robberies are done at night after bedtime; and it is truly amazing how, even though no one says a thing, everyone knows who did it. Ena, Neill's wife, usually doesn't make a stink about it. Instead, she puts the price of the stolen stuff on the bill as damages. As this is a standard item on all bills, parents are not unduly upset.

When I first came to Summerhill, I was put in a room with three big crooks. They frequently broke into the kitchen, and they invited me along. I really wanted to join, but I didn't have the nerve. So I usually just lay in bed waiting for them to return, content in the knowledge that I knew something the rest of the school didn't.

Most kids weren't very careful about cleaning up properly after gorging themselves. Invariably, crumbs of cookies, etc. were found on the floor of the room of the guilty party, and he was exposed.

I only broke into the kitchen twice: once during my third year, and once during my fourth year. Not because I was a crook, but because I had a moral obligation to myself I had to fulfill. And when I had done it, my heart was at rest.

WHAT KIND OF A SCHOOL IS SUMMERHILL?

SUMMERHILL, in case you haven't gathered by now, is a "free" school which has been going on in England for 46 years. It runs on a basis of self-government. Everybody from the youngest child right up to Neill has an equal vote. Neill, the founder of Summerhill, is 86. His basic philosophy is that if a child is given love and complete approval to do as he pleases—provided that what he does is neither dangerous to himself nor annoying to others—then he will grow up to be a happier, more mature adult.

All lessons are optional. The idea is that if a child is allowed to play as long as he likes, when he finally decides he wants to learn something, the motivation is entirely his own.

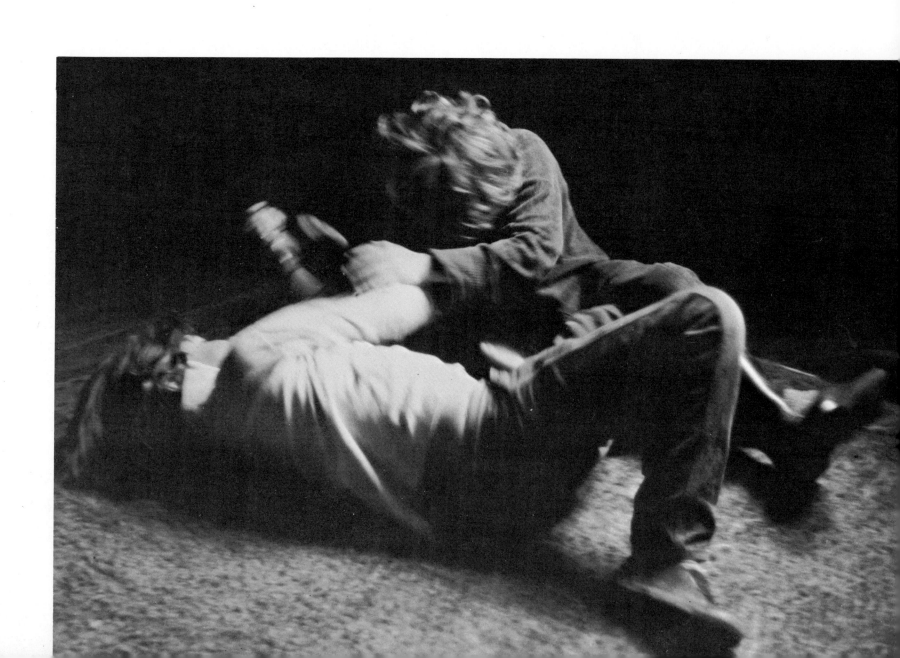

He will obviously learn more quickly and thoroughly this way than under force. There are no grades nor report cards.

At Summerhill, the emotions come before the intellect. Always! Helping a child to be happy in life is far more important than training him to be another Einstein.

FREEDOM—NOT LICENSE

SOME PEOPLE get the idea that because we are a free school, there are no rules, and that everyone does as he pleases. This is not so. When a person infringes in any way on someone else's rights, we don't consider that freedom. We have an incredibly long list of laws made by the community to protect the rights of others from inconsiderate people.

Moreover, there's a list of safety rules laid down by Neill and his wife, Ena. For example, one safety rule is that kids under a certain age may not possess matches or knives. These safety rules are arbitrary, and are not subject to change by the weekly General Meeting.

THE GENERAL MEETING is held on Saturday evening. All the school business, both general and personal, is discussed. Kids and teachers can make proposals about the school rules, or can bring a charge against another individual. Or anything else can be brought up. A vote is taken to settle the issue. Each student and each member of the staff has one vote. Attendance at the meeting is not compulsory, but most kids attend because they don't want any new laws passed behind their backs.

There is a secretary and a chairman at each meeting. The secretary is a volunteer who writes down all that happens in the meetings for future reference in the case of conflicting memories over a certain law. The secretary keeps the job for as long as he or she wants to. As far as I'm concerned, the job is a royal pain up the ass, because you have to be able to write very fast, and then be able to read your writing later on. The chairman changes each week, being picked during the week by the chairman of the previous week.

The chairman has the difficult job of keeping the meeting in order. He calls on those persons whose hands are raised, and he can fine or throw out anyone who is making a disturbance. To be chairman is a most difficult task, because most of the small children soon lose patience. At first, they start to play with each

other and make noise. Then, they may decide to put on a performance for their convenient, built-in audience. And they are superbly stubborn about leaving. Being chairman is very frustrating. Several times, I seriously considered having those kids tied and locked up somewhere.

There is no strict seating order during the meeting; people are sprawled out in every imaginable position. Little children find loving arms wherever they sit. A nice scene.

THE BANK ROBBERIES AND HOW THEY WERE DEALT WITH

ONLY ONCE IN A great while *does* it stop being a nice scene. That happened only once in the entire four years I spent at Summerhill. Some of us became so angry we overstepped the rules and took the law into our own hands. It wasn't just a few kids who acted this way; the group included Neill's wife and some other members of the staff. Of course, it had been building up to this for the last couple of terms; the incredible scene was a showdown.

Eight-, nine-, and ten-year olds are the ones who usually disrupt things, and there are ways that the general meeting can handle them. One way is to reward the leader of the group, and to punish his gang. The punishment the meeting metes out is not nearly as severe as the word implies; it usually amounts to being fined a couple of pennies or having to clean up a section of the grounds. More often than not after being punished, these troublesome gangs will break up. But this one case was different.

A 14-year-old boy from Norway had come to the school a year earlier. He had been teased about his name by some 7- and 8-year olds. His natural reaction to this was to beat up these kids, which didn't exactly win him many friends. Even though he knew he could bring up a case against those molesting kids in the meeting, he put little faith in that course, and continued to use physical force. He was 14, as I said, and it was hard for him to overcome this warlike characteristic.

Anyway, he became alienated from the school, and he spent a lot of his time with the leather-jacket motorcycle types from the town. He always needed money to buy their friendship and to impress them. Since he didn't have any more money than the rest of the kids of his age, he had to steal to get it. A couple of 11- and 12-year old boys looking for excitement joined up with him, and the three of them together plotted all sorts of ingenious crimes. Their main type of burglary was stealing food from the kitchen and breaking into the school bank. Since everyone knew who had done it, the food or bank money was replaced, and the loss put on the bills of the guilty kids. However, the whole affair was especially annoying to the teacher in charge of the bank money, because in order to get to the money, the crooks had to break the window of his hut, and he disliked sleeping in the cold.

Slightly off the point, but interesting nevertheless, is the fact that during all this commotion, a boy of 15, who was a strong and valuable member of the community and always had been so, broke into the teacher's hut and stole several pounds sterling—which he voluntarily returned the next day. When asked why he had robbed the bank, he replied, "Because I thought the time was ripe." There were no evil thoughts in his head. He had been wanting to do something like that for years, and when he had gotten it out of his system, he went back to being an even better person than he was before. That act helped him a great deal, and undue punishment could have so easily destroyed him. That is the difference between Summerhill and a conventional environment. The moralists say that whatever the reason or outcome is, stealing is a sin, so a thief must be punished even for what was just curiosity of the moment. For such moralists, there is no exception of any kind. Summerhillians all knew what this guy had done; but instead

of persecuting him for it, they joked and laughed about it with him afterwards.

Now, getting back to my original story: Although bank and kitchen thefts were annoying, they were handled in the usual way. But the community really bared its fangs when these particular kids began to steal from other students and deliberately damaged other people's possessions. The meeting tried everything in its power. But the meeting didn't succeed in stopping this gang because these kids just didn't give a damn about the school or anyone in it. The only reason we had put up with them for a year was because of Neill's firm belief that all problems in a child are basically parental or environmental in origin, and that it is only a matter of time until the goodness in a child is reached by breaking away all the layers covering his better side. The older a person gets, however, the more indestructible this coating becomes, and the 14-year-old Norwegian boy never seemed to open himself to the benefits of Summerhill.

As tension grew, several incidents, occurring all in a period of about 24 hours, sparked off the final explosion.

The teacher who had been keeping the bank money got so fed up with having his room broken into that he announced—

rather foolishly I think—that he was locking the money in the loft above his room, and that anyone was welcome to try and take it.

This offer was too tempting for our young heroes to pass up. One night soon after, they broke in by climbing up to the roof, removing the shingles, and then climbing down into the loft. They took about £10 or $24.00, which at Summerhill is a fortune. At the same time, they broke into the kitchen and stole the keys which were hanging inside the door. Some of these keys were vital to the smooth functioning of the school. A day or so earlier, they had cleaned out the purse of our English teacher of about £3 which is around $7.20.

So when a special meeting was called—a meeting about something so important that it cannot wait until Saturday—everyone was furious and bloodthirsty. I was fortunate, or unfortunate, enough to be chairman that week, so I got a birdseye view of the entire proceedings. After hearing the usual denials, which by now were becoming an awful bore, one after another of the staff and the kids gave hellfire speeches about how long we had tolerated those bastards, and how many second chances they had been given. Tempers were now raging hot. When the guilty kids tried to leave the meeting—which is always anybody's undeniable privilege—they were forced to stay and listen. For we all agreed: why should we obey the rules of courtesy and democracy that the school had made when these kids had been ignoring these rules and abusing them for months.

As chairman, I had the power to dissolve the meeting. But I felt it would be a valuable experience to show these anti-social pupils that they could get away with murder up to a certain point—and no further! The toleration at Summerhill is vast. We had put up for a full year with bad behavior of a kind that an ordinary school would not have put up with for a week.

So, some of the staff held these kids down. I and some others went through their pockets. And we found the missing keys.

Then these kids started getting scared and confessed to all sorts of petty crimes done months ago. The Norwegian boy was expelled, and he left school a week or so later.

Neill hates sending anyone away, but the school would have fallen apart had he not agreed to our decision. In part, the boy's problem was our fault because of the way he was partially rejected when he first came to school.

As far as I know, this was the first incident of its kind in Summerhill's history, and it well may be the last.

THE PROBLEM OF VISITORS

As I wrote earlier, when I first visited Summerhill I wasn't exactly greeted with open arms, and I felt pretty bad about it. After being at Summerhill for a few terms, I realized why visitors were so often rebuffed, and I began to feel the same way towards them. As Summerhill is the original "free" school, Neill has many worshippers all over the world. On Saturdays and Sundays they descend on us, sometimes even outnumbering the entire school population. At first you feel kind of proud and important to know that all these people have come expressly to see how you live, but after months of being asked the same questions, the repetition gets to be quite a drag. Running an efficient school is hard enough, but having it turn into a zoo for two days every week is immensely disturbing to the animals. Ooops! I meant the occupants.

Although there are signs plastered all over the place telling visitors where they may or may not go—such as into private rooms without being invited—some people manage quite successfully to ignore the rules and they tramp into kids'

rooms. We would get involved in a brilliant discussion like:

> Q: *"How long have you been here?"*
> A: *"About eight years."*
> Q: *"Do you like it?"*

Questions like that last one—Well! I better not comment.

Occasionally, we would strike back in various ways. We would sometimes bombard the visitors with snowballs, or as once occurred when we were feeling a bit nastier, with soggy lumps of toilet paper. The funniest thing was how they reacted. They usually just took things in their stride, thinking how wonderful it was that we were so free and could express ourselves so easily.

THE ONE USEFUL SERVICE visitors do provide by their presence is that the kids can sell souvenirs and refreshments. This is how we earned money for our End-of-Term party. At one point, I was selling photographs of the school and of Neill to visitors to make money for the School Building Fund. That turned out to be an extremely profitable venture. Some visitors are so fanatically in love with the place that I'm confident we could sell them a packet of genuine Summerhill mud without much difficulty.

I just mentioned the End-of-Term party. It's an old custom at Summerhill; it merits some comment. I don't know for how many years we've had EOT parties, but I'm sure it's been for at least twenty.

A term is approximately three months long. About six weeks before we leave school, seven out of about 25 applicants are elected as the EOT committee. These seven members buy food and sell it to the rest of the kids at a profit.

Every Saturday after pocket money is given out, the EOT committee encourages kids to play penny games that have been set up to raise revenue. Most kids are quite amiable about spending money on these games because they know the proceeds go towards the EOT party.

The usual Summerhill garb for both girls and boys is a practical pair of jeans and a sweater. That's one of the unique things about Summerhill. People wear whatever they feel most comfortable in, and no one chastises them for it. EOT is the greatest opportunity the kids have to dress up and wear fancy clothing. The girls usually work for weeks to make clothes for EOT party. The needlework teacher often assists them.

But it is not by any means only the females who dress up for EOT. My brother, who was twelve at the time, made a beautiful turquoise corduroy suit with trousers and a vest, lined with pink silk.

One week before EOT, the committee, who have by now settled on a theme, go into the art room to start painting. All the materials have to be paid for by the £10 or so ($24) that have been earned. The art room is kept locked so that everything will come as a surprise. But there is usually some little bugger who finds out what the theme is, and he or she goes around trying to tell the secret to everyone, incurring dire threats from the committee.

The day before the party, the EOT committee closes up the lounge, moves in all the paintings, and then starts a day and a half of hysteria, fatigue, bitchiness, and pessimism, along with a lot of hard work. One EOT night, I was extremely fortunate to be allowed in the art room and lounge to photograph the goings on.

Finally, on the last Saturday before we leave, comes EOT Night. The housemothers work furiously to bathe and wash the hair of all their little kids so they will return home looking presentable. The EOT committee puts the final touches on their art, and works out a timetable of events for the evening.

The bulk of the EOT evening is usually taken up with dancing. By modern standards, Summerhill's record collection may be considered extremely inadequate, but it serves its purpose fairly well.

There is usually a floor show. In my earlier days at the school when there were a goodly number of 15, 16 and 17-year-old girls, a beautiful dance production was often presented. This was laboriously planned and detailed, and invariably resulted in a beautiful display of graceful bodies and physical harmony. For one such dance, the girls wore bikinis, and then covered themselves from head to toe with gold powder until they glistened. They then danced slowly and sensually in circular patterns to the song "Goldfinger."

Finally, as day sinks into evening, the time approaches for the plays to begin. Don't make the mistake of thinking that

we put on an annual production of Shakespeare, or anything like that. I do not remember having ever seen in my four years at Summerhill a proper play written by someone unconnected with Summerhill. All plays, skits, and sketches are written by the kids or by the staff, and the productions are almost always comedies. I think a bunch of kids would never tolerate a serious drama unless they were forced to listen. They demand livelier entertainment. Our plays were usually about witches, crooks, or funny situations in the school—with the characters played by the real people.

For instance, there is a housemother at Summerhill who has been there for years and years. I do not know of any term when she hasn't written a play. She always performs last; and she somehow incorporates the throwing out of candy to the audience as the last part of her play. Aware of what to expect, the littlest kids in the school usually crawl to the front of the hall on their hands and knees, and each is given a little bagful of candy before the plays start; otherwise, they might be trampled on and get none of the sweets amidst the thunderous assault on the candies that will come later.

At midnight, several things happen. The first is the drawing of raffle tickets by Neill. The prizes are generally a big basket of fruit, or a token with which one can select a record, or something like that.

One year, I won fourth prize. There was a monkey-shaped piñata hanging from the ceiling in the center of the lounge and my prize was the honor of taking the first strike. When a piñata is struck, it breaks open and lots of goodies fall out. To my great dismay, I was too short to reach the piñata, even with the aid of a long broomhandle. But by that stage of my life, my lack of height did not bother me the way it had earlier.

On EOT Night, Neill ritually complains about staying up so late; but he always stops grumbling to lead the school in holding hands and singing *Auld Lang Syne* to those students who are leaving. Invariably, there are floods of tears. It's a very emotional scene.

The rest of the evening—which by now is morning—is spent dancing and just being together. It is the only night of the term when kids can stay up indefinitely; and if you look around at about five of the morning after, you will always find little children asleep in cubby holes, after they've vainly tried to stay up the entire night.

Actually, in my last two terms, I was getting quite bored with the End-of-Term party because even though the theme of the decorations changed, the basic patterns and actions did not; and there was, to me at least, a distinct feeling of repetition. Several times, I made suggestions involving change, but my suggestions were virtually ignored. End-of-Term tradition is not easily broken. More's the pity!

Now that there is such a nice swimming pool, I thought it would be great to have an End-of-Term party for a whole day once a year at the end of the Summer Term. It could be held outdoors, and all the money that the End-of-Term Committee earned could go to buying food for a giant barbecue. People could just swim and have a good time. One drawback of the traditional End-of-Term party is that most of the ex-Summerhillians and parents who come to visit usually go down to the pub during the evening, coming back sloshed and unpleasant. Having the party during the day might hopefully narrow down that number, since many folks don't like to start drinking in the morning. I guess it's none of my business anymore, though, because I'm no longer a student at the school.

SCHOOL PLAYS

EOT IS NOT THE ONLY occasion for dramatic presentations. Plays are often put on. I remember once being in a gangster play written by Neill. After a couple of rehearsals, the rest of the cast and myself conferred. We then fired Neill as director for being too authoritarian. He had been demanding loud

speech and he had required certain precise movements. We then asked the English teacher to come and direct us. She did, and the play was a great success.

For me, the funniest and most entertaining plays are those performed by the youngest kids. Sometimes they are only four years old. Their plays have no structure and no rehearsed dialogue; the only continuity is in the general idea of the theme. They just get up on the stage, and virtually all they do is play, completely forgetting about the audience.

Every Sunday, Neill conducts a class in spontaneous acting. He thinks up a hypothetical situation; and without the use of any props, kids will volunteer to act it out. For example, he once suggested that someone pretend to be cracking open a safe in someone's store when Neill, acting as the owner, walks in and catches the thief red-handed. What would the thief do or say?

There have been some extremely clever answers to some of these situations. Unfortunately, in recent months, this activity has not been too successful due primarily to the great preponderance of very young kids at the school.

Sometimes on Sunday evenings, instead of a session of spontaneous acting, a discussion is held. This discussion is

INSIDE
SUMMERHILL
60

different from the general meeting because, as a rule, only the older kids are allowed to take part. The topics usually cover general rather than specific problems. There is much active participation in these discussions, partly because of Neill's habit of making some outrageous statement in order to get the participants to react heatedly.

THE SCHOOL POPULATION

THE SCHOOL IS GOING through a rather bad patch at the moment, as it does every five or six years when there are not enough older kids to keep the younger ones in check. In a school like Summerhill there has to be some sort of balance between the age groups, or disaster occurs. The concept of freedom without license is very hard to instil in very young kids; but if they come in contact with older people living that way, they are quick to follow the good example. That is why Neill tries not to accept anyone over eleven, because by that age, a person is usually pretty set in his ways. If he comes from a restrictive home, he may have a hard time adjusting to freedom, and he may make it hard for the school to function smoothly.

Neill has no way of screening kids who come from overseas. The parents write that their kid is sweet, bright, and the paragon of everything Summerhill would like to have. Quite frequently that kid turns out to be exactly the opposite. The parents were having such trouble at home with him, they were desperate about getting him admitted and simply didn't tell the truth. As Neill says over and over again, Summerhill is not a school for problem children. At least, it wasn't meant to be.

If they remain at Summerhill long enough, the current crop of small kids will turn out to be a fantastic bunch when they get a bit older. Not infrequently, parents take their kid out of Summerhill when he is about twelve, saying that he has played long enough, and that it is time to send him to a school where he will *learn* something. For two reasons, that is undeniable rubbish.

First of all, one is learning all the time. What a kid *wants* to learn may be entirely different from what his parents want him to know, but doesn't it seem logical that the person who has to do the learning should have the choice? Secondly, for those who are concerned with academic subjects, Summerhill offers anything that is required.

For example, I have just returned to the United States, and have entered the twelfth grade of high school. Most of the other kids in my new class are actually a year and two older than I am. Which proves that Summerhill does have the facilities for learning, but a kid needs to be pretty much self-motivated.

Dominique = un élève
Adrienne = une élève
Alleeee = une élève
Megan = une élève
Ruth =
Mercredi = Mercury-day
Jeudi = gamesday
Vendredi = Selling market day.
Samedi =

CLASSES

The Summerhill workshop is fantastically equipped; it is used by both sexes. Anything from basket-weaving to enameling and even guitar-making are among the activities. It is, by far, the most popular class at Summerhill.

The rest of the classes are not as well equipped, but little by little they, too, are being improved as funds develop.

The teachers are happy to teach you anything they know, even though what you request to be taught is not in the regular curriculum. During my last term, I was taught karate by a Welsh girl who happened to be my regular English teacher. I learned a bit of archery from my biology teacher.

GROUP ACTIVITIES

One of the things that's so nice about Summerhill is the mass participation in most activities. For instance, I remember a snowball fight a couple of years ago joined in by almost the entire school. Just the feeling of playing with everyone else was wonderful.

We are fortunate to have a swimming pool. It was built only two years ago, and is now both life and soul on a hot summer afternoon. The kids practically live in that pool. On a hot day the typical agenda is swimming before breakfast, after lunch, after tea-time, after supper, or at any other time when the pool is open. Most kids swim in the nude; there are no moral feelings about nudity, but a majority of the older boys don't go naked because of a physiological reaction beyond their control.

NEILL

WHEN I FIRST CAME to the school, Neill taught classes in English. But he gave that up because he felt too old to carry on, and he received numerous complaints from kids who seriously wanted to learn that subject. Neill was always inclined to spend time in English class joking and playing word games.

Today, he spends most of his time replying to the overwhelming numbers of people who write to him. They want information, request applications for admission, want permission to visit, and often send him requests to go on lecture tours. Every week he gets several letters from kids in America who, after stating their complaints about their schools and about their families, beg to be admitted. He gets very upset at having to turn down most of these kids, but he is determined

not to let the school enrollment exceed sixty. Things would begin to operate on a very impersonal level if Summerhill got too big.

This reminds me of an incredible hoax played on Neill quite recently.

I was walking along the hall one Saturday, and Neill poked his head out of his office door, and asked me to go look for an American couple who were waiting to see him. When I couldn't find them, I went back to his office and started to chat with him. He explained that a little girl had come up to him and said that her parents had told her she could come to the school, and how happy she was about it. He was waiting to talk to the parents. But it made him so mad, he told me, when parents raised the hopes of their kids, without first talking to him to find out if there was room in the school for their child. That particular term there was absolutely no chance to be accepted. At that point, with Neill intensely serious, in walked the little girl again. I could hardly stop myself from bursting out in laughter. The little girl was my twelve-year-old brother, wearing a dress, sucking his thumb, and talking in a high-pitched whine, with his face pointed towards the floor, and his head covered with a strategically placed scarf. Eventually, we let on to Neill and he was extremely amused—as well as thankful he wouldn't have to turn away that little girl.

If a kid is feeling miserable or having a problem, he goes and talks to Neill. For that matter, anybody in Summerhill will spend hours comforting or talking with someone who needs conversation or comfort.

Every year, before Ena's or Neill's birthday, a meeting is called at which we try to think of a suitable gift. We usually end up getting some liquor for Neill, and some plants for Ena.

On Ena's last birthday, we gave her something with a lot of feeling that I think she really appreciated. It was a photograph of all the kids in the school. She has seen so many kids come and go, but this was the first time she had all her charges in one picture. It was hardly the conventional school portrait of formal poses one normally sees in a school picture. Some kids held two fingers pointed up, palm inwards. This means something a lot coarser than peace. Unfortunately, I wasn't in the picture since I was taking it.

Neill is an extraordinarily gentle soul, and during my last couple of terms I used to chat with him quite a bit in his office. I was the oldest pupil at the school at that time, and we would discuss some of the school's problems and what could possibly be done to remedy them.

He loves to sit and talk for a spell. Once, a friend and I went over to his cottage at about nine-thirty one evening and we

started talking. We were still there at eleven-thirty, having become so absorbed that we missed our bedtime altogether. However, if we had been fined our breakfasts, Neill would have had to miss his as well, being an accessory to the crime. But luckily, we weren't fined.

Once, when I was looking at a collection of photographs of Neill taken over 30 years ago, he told me that if he hadn't started Summerhill or entered the field of education, he would have liked to have been an archeologist. There must be a connection there somewhere. Despite his age, he is extremely strong; his bear hug could practically kill you. In Neill, there is a golden flame that makes you feel warm when you're near him.

HOW THE KIDS SPEND THEIR DAYS

ALTHOUGH THE WHOLE philosophy and lack of structure in Summerhill make for anything but dull repetition, certain patterns of behavior manifest themselves throughout the usual day.

The breakfast bell is rung at 8:30 every morning, and most of the kids get out of bed and drag themselves to the serving hatch of the kitchen from which all the meals are served. It is an old tradition at Summerhill to grumble about the food;

but it is supposed to be better than what one gets in most English boarding schools.

Those who wish to skip breakfast and remain in bed can do so until 9:30, when the maids come in to make the beds and clean up. The older kids, and those with single or double rooms, usually do the cleaning up themselves.

The bell for the first class is rung at 9:30. Those who want to go, go. There are seven class periods a day; each is 40 minutes long. There are five scheduled in the morning, and two in the afternoon. When some girl and I were studying for our General Certificate of Education examinations, we attended a class held at 7:30 in the morning, before breakfast. These sessions were not overly successful because we couldn't keep our eyes open.

I would say that the average class in Summerhill is composed of about six students. For a time, I was the only person in the advanced biology class; I certainly couldn't complain of any lack of individual attention.

Classes are grouped by ability rather than age. There are normally five levels, each with an age span of two to three years, rather than the twelve grades of one year each, as in the American system. This allows for greater flexibility in placing kids where they will work best. Because of the small classes,

optional learning, and advancement through ability rather than age, Summerhill pupils usually take only two years to prepare for particular exams. Three or four years are generally spent in study of the same subject matter in the normal English schools.

During all classes there is wide latitude for any other topic of interest to emerge, even if it has nothing to do with the particular subject the class is supposed to be dealing with. No attempt is made by the teacher to stop the digression. He may choose to remind the students, however, that if they are following a particular schedule they ought to return to the original subject in order to complete the course within the estimated time limit.

The world history course which I attended with one other student seemed to turn, most of the time, into a course about current world affairs, a subject which interested us much more than world history. The only reason we attended the class on world history was because we were both leaving the school and we needed the academic credits to enter schools in our respective countries.

I see this as a dilemma between Summerhill's ideological objectives and the need to conform to an opposing system of education. Neill's philosophy holds that kids who are allowed to study whatever they please and are not pressured to learn a

subject will be happy and emotionally healthy. Personally, I agree with him; but the conventional form of education upon which society rests, does not. Society demands grades, report cards, credits, and little pieces of paper which confer intellectual status. In order for the average man to make a decent living today, he has to have these diplomas and degrees. Only certain people, highly talented in creative arts can support themselves without capitulation to the system. But they are only a few. I can't recall a single older student at Summerhill, myself included, who studied only the subjects he wanted to. All students in the upper classes had to take certain courses, *if* they wanted to prepare for college entrance. This, therefore, somewhat defeats an important Summerhill concept.

Now to get back to my account of the patterns present in a typical day.

The two classes which run from 9:30 until 10:50 are followed by a 20-minute break during which we receive our mail and get something to drink. At 11:10 we resume lessons, and there are then three more periods before the second lunch sitting at 1:15. Throughout this time, the kids who haven't gone to lessons have been doing whatever they feel like doing. They may be just playing, or lolling about or playing the phonograph.

After lunch, everyone is totally free. Whatever one does, depends on the weather: there's swimming in the summer, or throwing snow around in the winter. More importantly, what one does depends on what goes on inside one's head. It is terribly difficult for me to document spontaneous, unregimented behavior. The way one person acts in Summerhill sets no criterion for the actions of another.

Four o'clock is tea time. Tea and cookies are served. This is followed by two more classes which run from 4:30 until 6:10, with a 20-minute break in between. These afternoon lessons are usually the most unproductive periods of the day because, after the half-hour break, one doesn't feel much like going back to work. The same sentiment is expressed by most of the teachers as well. Not infrequently we would say, "Oh fuck it!", or some such other subtle words of wisdom, and then go outside and lie in the grass and talk of trifles.

Because of the lack of structure in Summerhill, kids who don't go to classes tend to treat the entire term as one unit, rather than 90 separate days, since the only time structure in their lives are meals and bedtime. At the moment, kids in Summerhill who don't go regularly to lessons probably constitute a majority. For many new students, this sudden freedom from classes develops patterns of anxiety which usually diminish as time goes by, and as they learn to cope with a non-structured environment. To put it simply, at Summerhill a kid is allowed to get absorbed in doing his thing without someone else telling him to stop and do something else.

INSIDE
SUMMERHILL
84

The second supper sitting takes place at 6:15. After mealtime, we have the rest of the evening free.

Lots of things happen in the evenings. We might go to the movies downtown, or play games in the lounge, or if it be Saturday night, attend the General Meeting, or attend drama class, or participate in a music appreciation group, or have just a discussion with Neill. Anyone is free at any time to organize anything he wants to; and if lots of people come, that's groovy.

At about 7:30, the very youngest kids go to bed. Bedtimes get progressively later for each age group. At 10:30, the oldest turn in. A boy who has his own room may read and work quietly in his room after bedtime, but this privilege is immediately revoked if he disturbs anyone.

BEDTIMES

At Summerhill, a big issue of conflict and debate occurs over the bedtimes. In any community of people where there is a wide range of ages, some will want or need more sleep than the others. So the problem is to find an arrangement that will allow these kids to go to bed early and sleep undisturbed. The difficulty is making sure that those who need less sleep keep quiet. This is a problem that is impossible to solve and still keep everybody happy.

It is an undeniable truth that when kids get together they make noise; so invariably, someone will be disturbed. We've tried all sorts of experiments, varying in strictness from imposing no bedtimes at all, to a strict patroling by bedtimes officers elected by the kids. For the first couple of days or so, the new law is kept beautifully. But gradually, people begin to think, "Well, it won't matter if only *I* get up, because *I* won't make any noise." So that kid gets up and prowls around the building until he meets some other kid and then they both start talking, very quickly forgetting to be quiet.

Theoretically, we might never impose bedtimes or any other rules if there were a majority against such rules; but fortunately, there are more than enough people who want to get a decent night's sleep. Actually, I don't think Ena and Neill would allow a rule for any great length of time of no bedtime for kids under a certain age, because sleep is so important for good health.

WHAT THE YOUNGEST CHILDREN DO

THE DAILY ROUTINE followed by the very youngest kids differs only slightly from that of the rest of the school. They are, of course, more dependent on their housemothers for simple functions such as bathing, getting their hair washed, and picking clean clothes to wear. Housemothers bathe their smallest kids together, and selection is always by convenience and not by sex.

The youngest children are knows as the *san kids* because the building they live in used to be a sanatorium. They eat breakfast and supper in their own building away from the rest of the school, but they eat lunch at the first sitting of the main dining room.

The curriculum of classes for these kids, ranging in age from approximately four to seven, is also structured differently from that of the rest of the school: instead of changing teachers for each class, they have only one teacher and have one classroom exclusively for their use. There are, however, set times when they can go into the workshop to make things, which turn into anything from guns to pinball machines.

When the weather is fine, much of their time is spent outdoors on nature walks, etc., or they may go on a bicycle ride to the nearby beach for a swim. When the san kids aren't in classes, they tend to spend a good deal of time in their housemother's room, playing games.

In the evening, it is quite customary for some of the older kids to help the san housemother put her children to bed.

As I see it, one of the nicest things about Summerhill for a small kid is the grounds, for there is enough space and woods for limitless adventure.

THE GROUNDS OF SUMMERHILL cover approximately eleven acres—lots of room to escape for anyone who wants to be alone. The younger boys love rolling around on the floor with each other, play fighting, and making one hell of a noise. So it is fortunate the grounds are big. There used to be a great hiding place in a little room under the ground. This room was reached by climbing down a little hole in the floor of the laundry room. Although this hiding place was off limits, it was constantly used until two clever jerks shat in some empty jam jars which were down there. The entrance was then boarded up.

Trees and tree huts have an immense popularity at Summerhill. One tree is called the "Big Beech," and has become an inseparable part of school life. A long rope hangs from one of its branches. After a boy has climbed about twenty feet up on the tree to a board nailed on two high branches, someone throws the rope up. It is a fantastic swing. After doing it once, you never want to quit. My mother always wished she had the guts to try it, but she never did.

INSIDE
SUMMERHILL
93

WHAT ROOM YOU ARE in is quite important to some kids. There are only a certain number of private rooms available and, of course, everyone covets one of these. These private rooms are usually occupied by the oldest kids and those who have been at the school for the longest time.

The tradition for at least twenty years was that the older boys lived in the "carriages," two old railroad cars about ten feet apart, around which a building and a roof had been constructed. There were six rooms in all. Some of these rooms were single; some, double.

Living in the carriages was the great dream of every boy at Summerhill. When we still lived in the main house, all of the boys of my age, those who were about ten and eleven, would take every opportunity to huddle around the heater in the center room of the carriages, just to feel as if he was one of the big lads.

After I was at the school for about two and one-half years, I shared a room in the carriages. A couple of terms later when I got a room to myself, I was really ecstatic. The custom is that once you get a room to yourself you keep it until you leave.

I had heard of no exception to the rule. And then they pulled the dirty trick of moving someone in with me. Naturally,

I was furious. But I soon realized there was no alternative; and since he was a nice kid, I didn't really mind that much after all.

In 1968, we had a big school inspection, and the inspectors didn't like the carriages for reasons of health. A replacement had to be built. The cheapest, easiest thing to put up was a prefab. It was pretty ugly; but we decorated our walls with lots of posters. This new building is still called the "carriages." It has nine rooms, and each room is occupied by only one person.

As in all such buildings, the walls are pretty thin. Recently, one boy, who was being constantly annoyed by some other kid, got really mad. He did not want to hit the kid who was badgering him, so he hit the wall of his room and punched a nice hole in it.

I miss the old carriages; they had a nice feeling about them. After tearing them down, we used the wood for a bonfire.

SUMMERHILL'S RELATIONSHIP WITH THE TOWN

THE GROUNDS ALSO INCLUDE a huge grass field where all sorts of activities take place, especially soccer. Recently, we played a group of men from Leiston, the town in which Summerhill is located. We lost two games and won two. While all the players on their team were more or less the same size, our players ranged from three to six feet. However, we had the advantage of having 20 to 30 kids on the sidelines, screaming in our favor.

Aside from soccer, our relationship with the "townies" was not what it should have been. Several times we were ignorantly referred to as the "free-fuck" school, which however unjust, did little to enhance Summerhill's reputation.

THE KIDS AND THE STAFF

ONE OF THE MOST beautiful aspects of Summerhill is the relationship between pupils and adults, a way of life that epitomizes all that Neill has been striving for. The kids and the staff have a casual manner toward each other, but in most cases, there is mutual respect. Anyone who puts on a more-superior-than-thou act doesn't last very long. When a teacher is accepted by Summerhill, he agrees to become an active participant in the community. Some of the teachers who have been fired in the past were those who felt no obligation to be with the kids, or to help them outside of class time. Being a teacher at Summerhill is a twenty-four hour job.

The Summerhill environment fosters creativity and self-expression. Almost all modern amenities that turn the average kid into a vegetable are missing at Summerhill. Kids have to rely on their own resourcefulness to keep busy. A kid absorbed in making a costume out of an old box is learning a lot more than a kid who is watching television for hours on end.

There *is* a television set at Summerhill, but watching it is strictly limited to a few hours a week. And it's mostly the kiddies' shows which are viewed since such shows give the kids and the teachers ideas about what things they can make.

SWEARING

SWEARING IN SUMMERHILL is as taken for granted as fish and chips are in England. The swearing upsets only those who are narrow-minded enough to classify certain words as good or bad. When I first came to Summerhill, I found it quite amusing to hear five-year-olds saying "fuck" and "shit." These, and other words like them, don't have any special connotation for these kids. To them "fuck" has no more meaning than "fiddle-dee-dee." The expression is only a habit. I was called Posh to rhyme with Josh, and three-quarters of the kids who called me "Posh" didn't have an inkling as to what that word meant.

One of our strictest rules is about not swearing downtown. Although we think the taboo ludicrous, we try to respect the feelings of the townspeople by not swearing in their presence.

SPECIAL ACTIVITIES

THE WAY SUMMERHILLIANS act at different times of the year
reflects the changing of the seasons. In the spring, summer, and
autumn, kids are much friendlier with each other, and there
are far less offense cases brought up than in the winter. This is
so because the kids spend most of their time outdoors during
the milder seasons. In the cold months, the kids stay indoors
more, and tend to get on each other's nerves.

At Summerhill, I learned to knit, and have made several
sweaters, using a fairly complicated technique with cable and
other stitches. Boys do not feel the slightest embarrassment at
doing what society says is only for girls. Conversely, every
summer the girls learn how to mend their bicycles.

THE GROUPS AT SUMMERHILL

THE SAME AS IN any community, Summerhill kids tend to divide
up into little gangs or cliques which exclude all others. I
remember, for instance, that a group of the older kids once
made buttons which declared the wearers were members of the
'in-crowd.' They strutted around and acted obnoxiously.

There always is a certain group of kids which the others would like to be part of. If you are not counted as part of that group, you hate all those who are in it; and if you happen to be in that group, you think you are the hottest shit this side of the Atlantic ocean.

I was in the coveted group for a time. It broke up when most of the kids who composed it left school. There were about six of us, and we used to sit all day in one of the girls' rooms drinking cocoa, and being first-class snobs.

There is an unusual and unfortunate phenomenon connected with being the school's in-crowd. We would break the bedtime laws like crazy, and we would never get punished in any way; while we would raise a storm if anyone else broke the same law. I've witnessed this sort of behavior countless times, and the only plausible explanation that I can think of why this behavior is tolerated is that many of the other kids are hoping they will get to join the groovy group at some later date, so they don't want to make enemies of the members.

There's another type of gang in Summerhill. It's the opposite from the in-group insofar as that the one is tight and exclusive, and the other changes just about as fast as is humanly possible. This second type of group is usually made up of the smallest kids. They charge around playing all sorts of active games in which everyone ends up filthy, and invariably, someone is hurt in some minor way. Occasionally, a group of, say, six kids realize what a great power of disruption it possesses, and that group goes around stealing, annoying, and bullying.

A number of tactics can be used to break up a gang of this sort. A very successful maneuver is for the General Meeting to reward the leader *and punish his gang*. The gang certainly won't hang together much longer after that.

My brother once told me about a gang he was in for a time. It was a great power trip for the 14-year-old boy who was the leader. All the members of the group were about 10 or 11 years old. Each member had to address the leader as *Flag-Master*, giving him the Nazi salute whenever he was met.

They held their meetings down in a coal cellar—very mysterious—and he would order them to do all sorts of things, like not eat anything all day, or to run through the woods while he set traps to catch them. Apparently, the only benefits the members got were pieces of candy he gave them now and again, and they were compelled to observe secrecy under all sorts of dire threats. Weird.

CREATIVITY

SUMMERHILLIANS are wildly enthusiastic and creative about writing. Here there are no limits. Writing at Summerhill is total self-expression. In a more conventional environment, a child is forced to consider style, structure, length, punctuation, plot formation and grammar. These restrictions can retard creativity, and the child probably distorts what he wanted to say in the first place. Such structured writing is intellectual rather than emotional. By contrast, I present some worthy examples of Summerhill verse.

Blue cherries and
cinnamon colored lilacs
engraved on an ivory
forest occur only
in the minds of happy people.
Great ladies in gowns
with cherry blossoms in their hair
can only be seen when
you look very closely.
    Dark walls and daggers
are far more easily
found, and awakening to life
can be very gray.

MICHELLE DUHRSSEN (14)

I swung on the lightbulb
And crashed into the wall
And clobbered a man
Twenty feet tall.

RUTH HYDE (11)

Gallows, garage, garbage, garment, gas,
Still there is time to wipe my ass.
Gold, goblin, golf, and gone,
Don't you think it's lots of fun.
Oblige me, do, and you will see
It's time for a cup of tea.
February is not good—
It is time for Yorks pud.
Nina is one of the staff;
she is green;
she must eat grass.

CATHY HYDE (13)

Most of the writing is a reflection of life in the school. Some good examples are poems written following Guy Fawkes night.

Guy Fawkes was an Englishman who tried to blow up the Houses of Parliament in the reign of King James I. He was caught just in time. Every year since then, on November 5th, huge bonfires are lit throughout England, and an effigy, aptly called "The Guy," are burnt. This celebration is comparable to our July Fourth fireworks and rockets. Since Summerhill doesn't celebrate Hallowe'en or Thanksgiving or the Fourth of July, Guy Fawkes Night is a big thing at the school. Everybody usually helps to collect wood for the bonfire.

Last year, the science teacher figured out a spectacular method of lighting the bonfire by chemical explosion. Unfortunately, the explosion went off as he was in the midst of setting it up, so only three kids, including me, saw the big blaze. Here are some poems written after Guy Fawkes day:

Flash bombs and Catherine wheels,
Mine of serpents shoot like eels,
*   The bonfire flames up high.*
The rockets shoot up. How they fly!
The rockets burst into stars.
Others look like going to Mars.

They whoosh up in colorful sparks.
People eat nice things like jam tarts.

DUNCAN BAGSHAW (13)

On November the Fifth,
fireworks bang,
and Catherine wheels hiss
in a pattern of vibrant attractive colours.
Yet it seems so sad
to hear the crack
and a scream of flame
and a scream of pain.

And then the alarm bells ring
to signal the horror of a firework flame—
and someone to blame.
As the doors open,
it wheels out in the middle of the night
with siren going
and danger lights flashing.
And it goes on its way
to the scene of a flame
that caused a blame
and the horror of a child aflame.
Oh, poor fireman, hard as it is,
I think it would be easier without this day,
without this night.

On that, be careful with firework bang
and firework flame
and don't give yourselves a fright.
Instead, give them to someone
who is careful with light
and make sure he or she is sensible tonight,
and remember the dangers of firework night.
Yet we enjoy a bang at night
And a fizzle of bright yellow, orange, and white;
enjoy the fun of a fountain of light
on that wondrous night.

SIMON EDWARDS (15)

All these selections appeared in "The Kite", the school paper which is hung on the bulletin wall whenever there are enough contributions.

In conclusion, my four years at Summerhill traced the sort of life I wish I could lead always. If everyone went to a school like Summerhill, and followed its philosophy, the world would no longer be made up of stereotyped plastic people who conform to their nation's ideals rather than their own. Their souls have been lost in the glove compartments of their annually new, annually bigger, and annually more powerful automobiles.

Each child is the only person on this earth who knows what is best for himself, and no one has the right to act as his boss, for that will inevitably harm rather than help the child's emotional development. More and more people are coming to realize this as the truth. But unfortunately, the power is held by those who think differently, and undoubtedly a great many years will pass before a complete change is made to a natural and humane form of education.

INSIDE
SUMMERHILL
111